DEDICATION

This book is dedicated to Papa Obafemi Oyeniyi Awolowo, Chief Olabode Akanbi Thomas, Leader and Deputy Leader of the Action Group, respectively; and all other leaders and members of that great Party that decisively won the Western House of Assembly elections of 1951 and thereby set up in that Region, a government whose record of achievements is second to none on the African Continent.

CONTENTS

ACKNOWLEDGEMENTS

ON TUESDAY 17 October 1989, my telephone rang. It was from our beloved Papa, the Late Alhaji S. O. Gbadamosi. He had just read my rejoinder in the *Nigerian Tribune* of that date to the attack of Dr. K.O. Mbadiwe on the leaders of the Action Group as published in *The Guardian* newspaper of 21 September 1989.

He, the great Alhaji, showered praises and prayers on me for the rejoinder which he considered very fitting. He urged me to write more.

In the afternoon of the same day, Papa Alfred O. Rewane, the *Osibakoro* of blessed memory, invited me to his office to commend the rejoinder.

His bosom friend, Otunba Solanke Onasanya, was with him and he too expressed his happiness with me for the exercise.

They too asked me to always find time to write more of such articles. Papa Rewane then invited me for tea and dinner on that same day. I had both and more in his Ikeja residence.

On Friday 27 of October 1989, Mr. Anthony Oladipo Adegbite, a one-time teacher and later on, a senior official of the P & T Department, got through to me on telephone and added his own kudos for the same rejoinder.

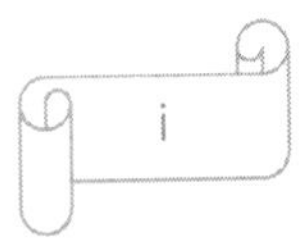

Mr. Adegbite is a long-time friend, much older and one of those who encouraged my active participation in politics in the early fifties. He was kind enough to read the manuscript of this work and made useful suggestions. Senator Abraham Adesanya and Samuel Ayo Adebanjo, my cell-mates during our period of incarceration in 1996, found time in a most difficult environment, to read the manuscript and give useful suggestions.

Other friends and colleagues who read the manuscript and also commended it and offered pieces of advice are Olaniwun Ajayi, E.O. Ferreira, Senator C.O. Adebayo and Chief Samuel Olu Falae.

The title exercise took me to a few libraries and archives for confirmation of some facts.

Mama H.I.D. Awolowo and Prince Oluwole Awolowo made it very easy for me to go in and out of Sopolu Library, in Ikenne, as many times as I liked.

The staff of the Ogun State University attached to the library were also very helpful. Next was the *Daily Times* library, in Agidingbi area of Ikeja, where Mr. E. Olatunji Okegbola, the Chief librarian, was fantastic in the way he rendered assistance.

Finally, I was at the National Archives, Ibadan, where I came in contact with Mr. Abiodun Afolabi,. He and his well-trained staff made my visit not only very successful but also memorable.

Miss Muibat Toyin Ajao is my young secretary. She and others, arranged by my son, G Olusegun Dawodu, had to type and retype the manuscript.

To all those mentioned above and others too numerous to list here, both dead or alive, I owe the realization of this effort. I am very grateful to them all.

FOREWORD

THIS CONTRIBUTION ARISES from the needless controversy surrounding the general elections in the Western Region in 1951, culminating in a series of unsubstantiated claims and reports about the political operators in the Region. Before now, there was no down-to-earth post mortem of the events except to heap unfounded accusations on the ruling party in the Region by its adversaries. This need not be so. The question then arises: *Awo or Zik: Who won the 1951 Western Nigeria Elections.*

Some of the attributes of this book can be found in the author's mission to destroy ethnic suspicion arising from prejudice in the political foundation of the Nigerian Nation.

Secondly, the work achieves the goal of establishing that the architects of the Action Group (AG) were not guided by base instincts but by a sincere desire to serve the people and therefore needed no Machiavellian propaganda to embark on a *Pseudo political* war against its peers.

Thirdly, the *dramatis personae* of the AG have been righteously discharged and acquitted of charges of disdain and the unwholesome stories woven around the Yoruba in Nigeria, nay in the Diaspora, among whom were numbered the leaders of the AG, as a people who

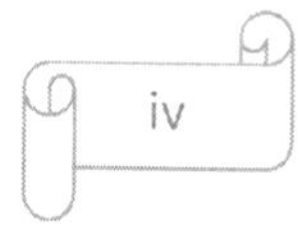

would sell out or even betray mutual confidence at the flimsiest opportunity.

Fourthly, the book provides inspiration for political science students and political leaders alike for them to drink from the water of wisdom springing from the deliberate and determinate and the undaunted will of the AG leadership to ensure the survival of the Party in spite of orchestrated antagonism and impediments in the political environment as clearly analyzed in the book.

In addition, the author is right in his challenge to political antagonists of the AG leadership and their cronies to discharge the onus of proof on their allegations against the AG or forever stop their blackmail.

This work came 45 years after the events on which the fructification of the leadership of the AG had been openly and clandestinely canvassed. The time lag has inexorably denied a whole generation the revelation of facts contained in it. Nonetheless, it serves the current and sustained generations as one good source to tap in the sincere search, quest and chart for a national discourse, knitting, and mouldcasting. The syntheses of the author are eloquent, credible and commendable. He, Alhaji Ganiyu O Dawodu, on the side of history, watched from the ringside of the political arena. He commented with the useful assistance of the referees of the limited but largely non-partisan daily newspapers of the time and arrived at a lucid, rational and logical

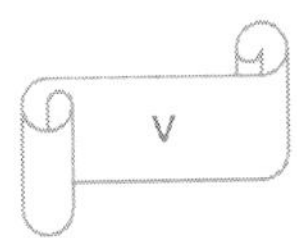

conclusion. I commend this work to all Nigerians and their friends worldwide.

Michael Adekunle Ajasin CFR
Owo, Nigeria.
23 August 1997

PREFACE

IN 1951, THERE were elections into the three Regional legislatures existing in Nigeria at that time. These were the Eastern, Western and Northern Houses of Assembly. The National Council of Nigeria and the Cameroons known for short as the NCNC and the Northern People's Congress, the NPC, had no difficulty in controlling the Eastern and Northern Houses, respectively. As a matter of fact, there were little or no political contests in the two Regions. Many of those who won were independent candidates, but as there was one strong and dominant party in each of the two Regions; there was no problem of the two parties gaining control of the two legislatures.

However, in the West, the electoral contest was fierce and keen between the Action Group of Nigeria and the National Council of Nigeria and the Cameroons, later known as the National Council of Nigerian Citizens. The election was clearly and decisively won by the Action Group but the NCNC leaders not only refused to concede victory but also put across the misrepresentation that they were the winners and that their victory was 'overturned' or 'stolen' from them. They used all means at their disposal to drum their calculated falsehood into the ears of their members and supporters, particularly those from the Eastern part of our great country.

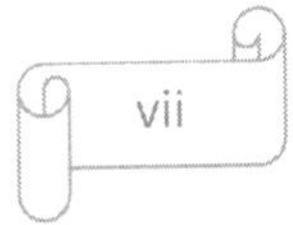

In undertaking this work, I seek to achieve three things.

The first is to put the records straight and educate or enlighten many Nigerians, who have had the facts of the results of the 1951 Western elections misrepresented to them.

The second reason is to protect the reputation of the dedicated leaders of the Action Group who fought and won a decisive and well-deserved electoral victory which their unsportsmanlike opponents have chosen to deride and misrepresent to the world.

The third and the least motive is that having erased the wrong notion that Dr. Nnamdi Azikiwe and his NCNC were robbed of victory in the 1951 election in the West, to seek to promote a new feeling of understanding, unity friendship, brother-hood and cooperation among Nigerians especially those in the East and the West.

Quotes:

Search for the truth is the noblest occupation of man: its publication is a duty.

- **Mme De Stael**

Truth crushed to earth will rise again:
The eternal years of God are hers:
But error wounded writhes in pain.
And dies amid her worshippers.

- **William Cullen Bryant**

Who speaks the truth stabs falsehood to the heart
--James Russel Lowell

The greatest friend of truth is time:
Her greatest enemy is prejudice.

- **CC Calton**

Falsehood may have its hour, but it has no future.

- **Francois D Presence**

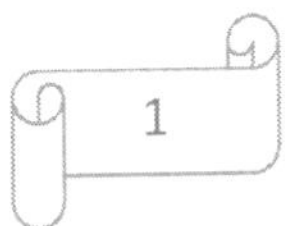

1

NCNC's Allegations --- against the Action Group on 1951 Western Regional election

BEFORE I go to the meat of this work which is to prove conclusively that the Action Group won decisively the Western Regional elections of 1951, it is necessary to recap the allegations of the NCNC leaders and their supporters in respect of the elections.

Dr. Kingsley Ozumba Mbadiwe, who was noted throughout his political career for making flamboyant statements and allegations without bothering to substantiate them, was the most vicious accuser of the Action Group leadership of everything evil in respect of 1951 parliamentary elections. His name would readily come to mind because of his many attacks some of which I wish to refer to.

In this autobiography titled, *"Rebirth of a Nation"*, Dr. Mbadiwe wrote in the last paragraph of page 71 of the book as follows.

"But in pursuance of the policy of creating a political climate healthy enough to make one a citizen wherever he lives, Dr. Azikiwe contested and won the general elections in 1951 into the Western House of Assembly. To stultify this policy of one Nigeria in favor of his tribally-based philosophy, Chief Awolowo got some elected members to cross the 'carpet' from the NCNC to his AG side. Zik the victor lost and Awolowo's party was able to form the government of the Western Region".

I also like to refer to another statement by Dr. Mbadiwe, this time on page 75 of the same book, where he asserted as follows:

"In the Western Region, the NCNC won the elections over the Action Group by a handsome majority. Here began the great

innovation and surprise in Nigeria elections hinted earlier. A most dangerous practice in the electoral process of Nigeria was introduced for the first time, namely carpet-crossing and open bribery, which were brought into operation by the Action Group. Overnight, successful NCNC members were bought over by the Action Group and the majority was reversed in its favor. Embers of tribalism were fanned by the Action Group leadership. Successful NCNC men who were not Yoruba were scared away. Dr. Azikiwe who won a seat to the Western House Assembly from a Lagos constituency, decided to resign. Since membership of the House of Representative was by an electoral college in the Regional house, no NCNC from the West came to the House of Representatives in Lagos. That was how Awolowo and his team qualified for the Federal House and Zik was therefore excluded."

In addition to the two statement quoted above, the late Dr. Mbadiwe, a former Federal Minister and prominent leader of the NCNC, addressed the press, on his 'vision' of the Third Republic on Wednesday 20 September 1989. During the course of this press conference, he launched another attack on the Late Chief Obafemi Awolowo and his party and accused them of introducing carpet-crossing into Nigerian politics. He also repeated his false claim that it was the NCNC and not the Action Group that won the first parliamentary elections to the Western House of Assembly in 1951.

I wish to quote what he said on that occasion as reported in *The Guardian* of Thursday 21 September 1989. Said he:

"Dr Azikiwe and his party won the majority of seats in the Western House of Assembly. He was due to be elected the Leader of Government Business, when overnight, the Action Group introduced the notorious carpet-crossing. By this manipulation, members who won under the NCNC crossed over to the Action Group building it to become the majority party in the West. As a result of this,

Chief Awolowo was elected Leader of Government Business and Dr. Azikiwe had to resign."

Comment

Each of the three statements of the late Elder Statesman quoted above, with due regard to his political status and memory, is to say the least, the very opposite of the truth. It is a classic example of what is known in legal parlance as *EXPRESSIO FALSI SUPPRESSIO VERI.*

When the last statement quoted above was published on the 21 September 1989, the author wrote a rejoinder which was published in the *Nigerian Tribune* of Tuesday, October 17, 1989, *with the title "History, Politics and the Nigerian Nation"; the Guardian and Vanguard* of Friday October 20, 1989 with the headlines *"Mbadiwe and the 1951 Western Elections" and K.O. Mbadiwe and the 1951 Western Region Elections, between Fact and Fiction"* respectively. The *Daily Sketch* also ran the story with the caption: "Rejoinder: Mbadiwe's great falsification," on Friday 27 October 1989.

The rejoinder published in four dailies on three different dates given above contained, in an abridged form, the facts put across in this work.

In the rejoinder, I explained why I had to write as follows: "In the interest of truth and accurate record of events and in order to educate many who might have been misled either in the past because of such past untrue statements by other NCNC leaders or by the one under reference, I like to give the facts, which I am sure will convince an unbiased person of the inaccuracies of Dr. Mbadiwe's assertions which are a falsification of events".

On that occasion, I ended the rejoinder thus: "In conclusion, I hasten to say that looking at all problems confronting our great country as at now and the need to promote peace,

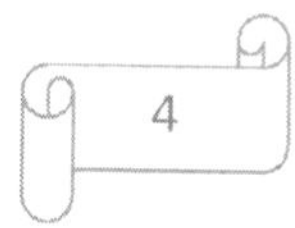

understanding and harmony among all Nigerians, one would find it very difficult to appreciate the relevance of the statement credited to Dr. Mbadiwe, an elder statesman. But be that as it may, one hopes that Dr. Mbadiwe and his associates, who have been peddling this false statement over the years, will show greater respect for the truth especially during these periods when important events are being chronicled for the benefit of future generations".

Readers would observe that all the statements of Dr. Mbadiwe quoted above contained only claims, assertions, and allegations. There was no attempt to prove anything and no evidence to back up any claim and allegations.

Of course, it is not just enough to accuse, the onus of proof remains the burden of the accuser. In other words, he who asserts must prove.

Dr. Mbadiwe in his life time failed to take up the challenge to prove or substantiate his accusations as has been done by this writer. The effect of his refusal or failure discredits his orchestrated false accusation eternally.

Carpet-Crossing

Let me say a few words about this. Carpet-crossing by a legislator to party B after winning an election on the platform of party A is a condemnable act. It is obtaining votes under false pretense.

However, a candidate who wins an election as an independent candidate can, in good conscience, join a political party, if he has good reasons to do so. It is better still if he has the support of the majority of his constituents.

Furthermore, carpet-crossing in the sense of changing a party badge for another is not a bad act per se. It may be based on principle or be due to change of policy or belief by either the candidate or his party.

After all, the great Winston Churchill of the United Kingdom was once a liberal before he became a Tory. Dr. Nnamdi Azikiwe too was a member of Nigerian Youth Movement before he crossed over to Herbert Macaulay's Nigerian National Democratic Party (NNDP).

Mbadiwe's Allegations Answered

Before I comment further, let me arrange serially the salient points in the three statements of Dr. Mbadiwe quote above. They are:

(a) That it was Zik and his party, the NCNC, that won the 1951 elections into the Western House of Assembly with a "handsome majority";
(b) That it was Awo and his party that induced through "open bribery", successful NCNC members to cross the carpet to the AG side overnight and thereby made it to become the majority party;
(c) That it was because of the "electoral robbery" that Zik left the West for the East;
(d) That successful NCNC members who were not Yoruba were "scared away";
(e) That because membership of the House of Representatives was by an electoral college system in the Regional house, no NCNC member went to the House of Representatives in Lagos from the West.

I will deal with these allegations one by one:

(a) We were told in the various statements of Dr Mbadiwe that the NCNC won the 1951 parliamentary elections in the West, by a "hand-some majority". Can any protagonist or supporter of this view define "hand-some majority"? How many seats did they win and from which divisions? What are the names of their successful candidates? I hereby affirm that the NCNC did not win the 1951 Western Parliamentary elections; it lost to the Action Group and I will prove this in the subsequent chapters of this work.

(b) If the NCNC lost the elections of 1951 to the Action Group as I know surely they did, the charge of inducement through "open bribery" to successful NCNC members to cross the carpet overnight must be a figment of the imagination of someone.

(c) As regards Zik's departure to the East for greener political pasture, the grand old man did so in order to be politically relevant and also to be able to exercise control over his party colleagues in the East over whom he was losing grips. So, Professor Eyo Ita and his government in the East had to be sacrificed for a new parliamentary election to take place to enable Zik to come in.

(d) By the time the Western House of Assembly met for the first time in January 1952, there were only four non-Yoruba members of the House on the Action Group side. They were Chiefs Arthur Prest, Anthony Enahoro, S.O. Ighodaro and M.F. Agidee. All the others like Dennis Osadebay, H Omo-Osagie, Festus Okotie-Eboh, Chike Ekwuyasi, Fidelis H. Utomi, Obi-Osagie, Yamu-Numa, G.O. Oweh and G.B. Ometan were on the side of the NCNC. How were they "scared away" and to where? Nobody was "scared away".

(e) As regards the assertion that no NCNC member was voted to the House of Representatives from the Western House, this is either a mistake or calculated falsehood. Dr Ibiyinka Olorun-Nimbe, Prince Adeleke Adedoyin, Chief Dennis Osadebay, Chief Frank Oputa-Otutu and Sir Odeleye Fadahunsi were voted from the West to the House of Representatives in 1952. Or were they not members of the NCNC? Of course, they were.

Other misrepresentations corrected

Another statement I wish to refer to is from a gentleman known as Paul Ukpo who was reported on 17 March 1994, in *The Guardian* to have spoken at a forum organized by Nigerian Union of Teachers in Enugu.

He was quoted to have traced the problem of the East to the "annulment of Dr Nnamdi Azikiwe's election as Premier in the Western House of Assembly, leading eventually to the intervention of the military into politics in 1966". Is this palpable ignorance or another calculated falsehood? When and how did Zik win the Premiership election in the West? How and by whom was it annulled? None of these things happened.

A regular contributor to *The Guardian,* Mr Charles Njoku, in one of his contributions in the paper once argued that since the NCNC won more seats than the AG from the West in the House of Representatives election of 1954, one must give credence to the NCNC claim of victory in 1951.

What sort of reasoning is this? We do not need to quote examples outside our country to puncture this argument. Does this writer know that the NCNC and its allies won the 1950 Lagos Town Council elections beating the AG and its allies by 18 to 6 seats?

The NCNC and its allies also won all the five Western House of Assembly seats from Lagos in 1951, beating their opponents of the AG massively. However, in the Lagos Town Council elections of 1953, the AG shocked the NCNC at the polls by 26 to 15 seats.

What would have been the reaction of Mr Njoku if someone had come out to argue that the NCNC could not have won the 1950 and 1951 elections because they lost the 1953 one? Are there not many factors which affect the fortunes of political parties in electoral contests year in year out?

The reasons why the Action Group narrowly lost the 1954 Federal election in the West are known to those who cared to find out. They had to do with the implementation of some aspects of the policy papers of the party which the House of Assembly had accepted as government program of work for implementation.

These were: (i) agricultural development including rubber plantation; (ii) customary court reforms (iii) democratization of local government councils and (iv) free universal primary education and free health service. All these had a great share in the electoral set-back of the Action Group in 1954. It is necessary to explain how.

Agricultural development

This beneficial scheme could not be achieved without land and this led the government to acquire either voluntarily or compulsorily, thousands of hectares of land especially for rubber plantation.

The owners of the acquired land felt deprived and were therefore very cross with the government and leaders of the party controlling it.

Many of the land owners demonstrated their annoyance at the 1954 Federal elections by voting against the Action Group.

Customary Court Reforms

Before the Action Group came to power in Western Nigeria, most of the customary court presidents and members were old and illiterate chiefs and other dignitaries.

There were also touts in the various court premises. The government in November 1953 enacted a law which enabled it to replace the illiterate court presidents with literate ones and also to ban touts from court premises. This was the law that led Alhaji Adegoke Adelabu to form his Mabolaje/NCNC

Alliance, which gained the support of the displaced chiefs and other dignitaries in Ibadan division.

This incident more than anything else, enhanced the popularity of Alhaji Adelabu in Ibadan because he capitalized greatly on the court reforms among the Chiefs and illiterate elders. Alhaji Adelabu was for many years the Leader of Opposition in the West.

Democratization of Local Government Councils

By 1951 when the Action Group was voted into office in the West, only one council – the Municipal Council of the city of Lagos – was already democratized. Its total membership of 24 had been elected since 1950. All the other councils throughout the country had more nominated or handpicked members than elected ones.

In 1953, as a result of a new law, the council in the West became largely democratic. Majority of councilors or members were elected and this displeased those who had been used to being nominated and they showed their displeasure in the 1954 Federal polls in the West by voting against the Action Group.

Free Universal Education and Free Health Service

When the free education service of the AG was planned, there was the debate as regards whether it should be compulsory or voluntary. A number of leaders of the party including Chief Awolowo were of the view that while the scheme should be free as planned it should be voluntary, while others, mostly the younger elements, wanted it free and compulsory.

Shortly before implementation began, the party members met to deliberate on the issue and those who wanted it made compulsory won the day. This decision was only reviewed after the 1954 Federal elections, when many members of the farming population who feared they might lose completely the services of their children and wards if the scheme was made compulsory, voted against the party.

Furthermore, it was necessary to raise some money to meet the cost of the free education and free health service. The Government therefore decided to call on the people of the region to make some sacrifice.

An education and health levy, otherwise known as capitation tax, of 10 shillings was fixed to be paid by every taxable adult. The proposal was taken to the House of Assembly for full dress marathon debate; members of the governing party did their best to win the support of the Opposition for the education and health levy which was to aid the implementation of that noble scheme without success.

As a matter of fact, members of the Opposition rose like one man, not only against but also used the forum to incite and indulge in wild propaganda against it.

Some of them openly told a lie that the levy was imposed to enable ministers to build houses and buy more flashy cars for themselves.

The author was in the public gallery on the last day of the debate and he listened to Chief Awolowo, the Leader of Government Business, who wound up the debate in a moving tone, as follows:

"We of the Action Group will press forward in the execution of the laudable project which this House has unanimously approved and accepted; believing as we do that God Almighty, who sees our hearts and knows that we are doing all these things to better the lot of our people is on our side; and confident that our beloved and trusting masses, once they begin to realize the fruits of the education and health levy, which they are now being called upon to pay, will now and in future years, remember us with gratitude and adoration and as their only true friends and benefactors.

Mr. President, Sir, I beg to move."

When the levy was imposed, it led to riots in many areas of the West because people were incited and instigated, but they paid at last. In 1954, the Action Group lost votes and parliamentary seats as a result. This electoral loss later became a plus for the party because it is the only instance on record that a government in power was defeated in a Parliamentary election organized or supervised by it in our country.

Furthermore, the Action Group government launched the free education and health service in 1955 and won the 1956 Regional elections by 48 to 32 seats and also won the subsequent ones in the Region.

More importantly, Awo's prophesy on the floor of the House, came true.

Why most references in this work are to the *Daily Times*

Before we move to the next chapter, I consider it necessary to direct readers' attention to the fact that most of the references in this work to reports in the dailies, are to the *Daily Times.*

This is deliberate and there are compelling reasons for it. I hereby give them.

The *Daily Times* is the oldest of the Nigerian dailies then and now. In terms of management, structure and organization, manpower and quality of production, it was second to none at that time.

It had technical know-how and financial resources to back up its printing and publishing business.

Furthermore, it was a credible and dependable newspaper in those days and its circulation was the highest not only in Nigeria, but also in the whole of West Africa.

More importantly, it was the only daily newspaper that was not attached to any political party or group. It was independent.

2
The 1951 Election Battle

THE 1951 PARLIAMENTARY elections held under the Macpherson Constitution were conducted throughout Nigeria under the electoral college system which provided for elections in three stages – primary, intermediate and final. Lagos was the only exception in the West where there was direct adult tax suffrage. Even here, the system was not as simple and straight-forward as it is today. It was a multiple constituency system with the whole municipality of Lagos being regarded as a constituency with every voter having five votes.

The primary elections in the West started on the 13 August 1951 and did not end until the 30th of the same month. The intermediate and final stages were prolonged till about the end of September 1951. The Lagos election was held on November 20 while that of Benin came on the 6th of December ,1951 owing to the postponement brought about by communal unrest in the area.

The obnoxious electoral college system made the elections to drag on for too long. May I say, in passing, that on assuming power, Awo was the first head of government in Nigeria to abolish the electoral college system in his Region and to introduce instead direct universal adult suffrage and voting by symbols. He also introduced the single-member ward or constituency.

Two main political parties – the Action Group and the NCNC vied for supremacy in the West, although there were other local parties some of which were Ibadan People's Party and Ibadan Citizens' Council in Ibadan, Ondo Improvement League in Ondo, Otu Edo and Taxpayers' Association in Benin. There was also the Nigerian People's Congress led by the late Chief HO Davies QC, that was thought would feature very well in the electoral battle but ended without making any impact on the results either in Lagos or any part of the region.

Attempt to Check Electoral Controversy

As the electoral battle progressed and by the middle of September 1951, there had been claims and counter-claims in respect of the results of primary and secondary elections so far declared. The authorities took an interest, sought to nip the controversy in the bud and the then Public Relations Officer of the Nigerian Government, Mr. Harold Cooper, wrote to the parties contesting the elections to submit the lists of their candidates for the final elections.

The request of Mr. Cooper for submission of the lists of candidates by parties was very much publicized by the press. The *Daily Times,* for example, in the left- hand column of the front page of its issue of Friday 21 September 1951, covered the news as follows:

Parties to name candidates?

"The Public Relations Officer, Mr. Harold Cooper, has written to political parties contesting the elctions to make known names of their candidate for the final elections to the House of Assembly.

He told newsmen at a press conference that this would help his department to identify the party to which elected candidates belong when issuing press releases or broadcasting results of the final election on Monday, September 22. It is understood that letters have been dispatched to the secretariats of the NCNC, The Action Group, The Nigerian People's Congress and other parties contesting the elections."

The Action Group submitted its list of candidates while the NCNC did not submit or publish its own.

The Action Group list was released before the final elections and published in the *Daily Service* and the *Nigerian Tribune* on and before the 24 September 1951, the day of the final election in most parts of the West. The list was also published in the *Daily Times* on the day of the elections on its front and last pages. It contained 68 names. The full list of the Action Group candidates submitted to Mr. Cooper and published in the press on and before the 24 September 1951, is as follows:

Ijebu Remo Division---- *Obafemi Awolowo; M.S .Sowole*
Ijebu Ode Division------ *S. O. Awokoya, Rev. S.A. Banjo and V.D. Phillips.*
Oyo Division--------------*Chief Bode Thomas, Abiodun Akerele, A.B.P. Martins, T.A. Amao and S.B. Eyitayo.*
Osun Division---*S. L .Akintola, J.O .Adigun, J.O. Oroge, S.I. Ogunwale, I.A . Adejare, J.A.Ogunmuyiwa and S.O. Ola.*
Ondo Division-------------*P.A. Ladapo and G.A Deko.*
Okitipupa Division-------*Dr. L.B. Lebi, C.A. Tewe and S.O. Tubo.*
Epe Division---------------*S. L .Edu, A. B. Gbajumo, Obafemi Ajayi and C. A. Williams.*
Ikeja Division--------------*O. Akeredolu-Ale, O. Gbadamosi and F.O. Okuntola*
Badagry Division--------- *Chief C.D. Akran, Akinyemi Amosu and Rev. G.M. Fisher*
Egba Division--------------*J.F. Odunjo, Alhaji A.T .Ahmed, C.P.A. Cole, Rev. S.A .Daramola, Akintoye Tejuoso, S.B. Sobande, I.O. Delano, and A Adedamola.*
Egbado Division ----------*J .Ola Odebiyi, D.A. Fafunmi, Adebiyi Adejumo, A. Akin Illo and P.O. Otegbeye.*
Ife Division---------------- *Rev. S.A. Adeyefa, D.A. Ademiluyi, J.O. Opadina and S.O. Olagbaju*
Ekiti Division--------------*E.A. Babalola, Rev. J. Ade Ajayi, S.K . Familoni, S.A. Okeya and D. Atolagbe.*
Owo Division------------- *M.A. Ajasin, A.O. Ogedengbe, J.A. Agunloye, L.O .Omojola and R.A. Olusa*
Western Ijaw Division-- *Pere E.H.Sapre-Obi and M.F. Agidee.*
Ishan Division------------ *Anthony Enahoro*

Urhobo Division--------- *W.E. Mowarin, J.B. Ohwinbiri and J.D. Ifode*
Warri Division-------------*Arthur Prest and O. Otere.*
Kukuruku Division-------*D.J.I . Igenuma*

In a short statement which accompanied its list of candidates, the Action Group stated as follows:
"It will be observed that in some divisions, the number of candidates exceed the number of seats to which such divisions are entitled. In such cases, the members concerned have the permission of the Action group to be nominated as candidates on the platform of the Action Group".
This was by way of explanation.
All the 68 names on the AG list, except one, contested the elections. The only person whose name was very conspicuous on the list but did not contest the election was Chief M.A Ajasin. He withdrew in the interest of the solidarity of his party, the Action group, and unity of Owo Division.
Owo Division in 1951 did not only comprise the citizens of Owo but also those of Akoko and others, who were and still are in the majority. The Owo wanted Chief Ajasin as a legislator in the House of Assembly and the Olowo of Owo, Sir. Olateru Olagbegi, as a member of the House of Chiefs. And of course, the two dignitaries were, if voted in, ministerial materials.
The people of Akoko and others on the other hand, who because of their numerical strength, had a majority in the final electoral college and also among the traditional rulers, chiefs and council members in the division and therefore were in a position to dictate the tune both ways, did not want to be put at a disadvantage. Readers must bear in mind that every division at that time was a multiple-member constituency. There was no single-member constituency as it is the case today.

There were three seats in the division in the House of Assembly and Papa Ajasin did calculate that D.K. Olumofin could win one for the NCNC and if care was not taken, the remaining two, which should go the AG way, might be lost through vote-splitting. He, Chief Ajasin, therefore decided, in spite of the attraction of ministerial appointment, to make a sacrifice by with-drawing his candidature for A.O. Ogedengbe and R.A. Olusa to win the two seats. D.K. Olumofin, as predicted, won for the NCNC. By his sacrifice, Chief Ajasin also guaranteed Sir Olateru Olagbegi's seat in the House of Chiefs. Sir Olateru was subsequently made a minister without portfolio in the Western Region.

Chief Ajasin's noble gesture was deeply appreciated by all and sundry and in the direct Federal election of 1954, he was fully supported to become the representative of the division in the House of Representatives in Lagos.

I should add that one other point that influenced the decision of Chief Ajasin to withdraw in 1951 was that he knew it would give him more time to concentrate on the problems associated with the growth and development of Imade College, whose responsibility as a young institution had just been put on his shoulders as its principal.

3
The Election Results

MONDAY 24 SEPTEMBER 1951 was the D-day. Except in the Lagos and Benin divisions, final elections took place in all the divisions of Western Region. There were, in all, 80 seats in the House of Assembly. Lagos and Benin had five and three, respectively. In other words, there were 72 seats at stake on the 24 of September 1951. They were keenly contested.

The results came, in earnest, from all divisions where there were contests and showed the Action Group leading in many areas.

In accordance with its list of candidates, it had won all the seven Osun seats, all the five in Oyo, four of the five in Egba, the three in Egbado and two of four in Ekiti, all the two each in Ife, Ijebu-Remo, Badagry and Ikeja. The party also had one seat each out of the two in Ishan, Warri, Okitipupa and Western Ijaw divisions.

Prominent leaders of the AG already elected as at September 26 were Obafemi Awolowo, Bode Thomas, S.L. Akintola, Arthur Prest, Anthony Enahoro, Abiodun Akerele, the father of Hilario Babs Akerele.

Others whose successes were recorded included S.O. Gbadamosi, M.S. Sowole, J.F. Odunjo, S.L. Edu, J.A.O. Odebiyi, C.D. Akran, E.A. Babalola and others.

On Wednesday 26 September 1951, the *Daily Times*, among other media, reported the success of the AG as follows:

"As more results were received yesterday, a check by the candidates claimed by the Action Group revealed that the party was still leading. So far, 38 out of the 72 seat contested go to the Action Group."

The newspaper then ended the news about the election by publishing results in respect of Western Ijaw, Epe, Aboh, Owo, Ishan, Warri and some other divisions.

Two days later, that is, on Friday 28 September 1951 the same newspaper reported on the elections as follows:

Election Results

38 seats for Action Group

Excepting Benin Division where elections have been postponed owing to recent riots and Lagos where elections will not be held until November, final results of the elections into the Western House of Assembly have now been released. So far, according to the names of its candidates which were released prior to the election day, the Action Group has captured 38 of the 72 seats which were contested. The full list of the 38 Action Group – sponsored candidates that won the elections held on Monday 24 September 1951, is as follows:

***IJEBU-REMO**: Obafemi Awolowo; M.S. Sowole.*

***IJEBU ODE**: Rev. S.A. Banjo;S.O. Awokoya.*

***OYO**:Bode Thomas;Abiodun Akerele; A.B.P. Martins; T.A. Amao; S.B. Eyitayo.*

***OSUN**: S.L. Akintola; J.O. Adigun; J.A. Oroge;S.I. Ogunwale; I.A. Adejare; J.A. Ogunmuyia; S.O. Ola.*

***EGBA:** J. F. Odunjo; Alhaji A.T. Ahmed; Rev. S.A. Daramola; Prince A. Adedamola.*

***EGBADO(now YEWA)**:J. A. O. Odebiyi; D.A. Fafunmi; A. Akin Illo*

***EKITI**:E. A. Babalola; Rev. J. Ade Ajayi.*

***BADAGRY:** Chief C.D. Akran; Rev. G.M. Fisher*

***IKEJA:** S. O. Gbadamosi; Akeredolu-Ale;*

***IFE:** Rev. S.A. Adeyefa; S.O. Olagbaju*

***OWO:** A.O. Ogedengbe; R.A. Olusa;*

***EPE**: S.L. Edu.*

***OKITIPUPA**:C.A. Tewe;*

***WESTERN IJAW**: M.F. Agidee.*

***ISHAN:** Anthony Enahoro.*

***WARRI:** Arthur Prest*

In addition to the two main parties – the Action Group and the NCNC that contested the Western elections, there were, as mentioned earlier, other local or divisional parties and it is important to focus on the performance of three of them – Ibadan People's Party, Ondo Improvement League and Out Edo of Benin.

The IPP came tops in Ibadan Division. It won all the six seats at stake. The party's torch-bearers who won were the one and only A.M.A. Akinloye, wealthy Moyosore Aboderin, and Adegoke Adelabu who later became the political "lion of Ibadan".

Others were Chief D.T. Akinbiyi, (the illustrious father of Mr D.M.O. Akinbiyi, one time Lagos Town Clerk and Prince Jide Akinbiyi, a popular Lagos journalist), Chief S.O. Lanlehin whose son, Femi Lanlehin, later became a member of the House of Representatives representing an Ikeja constituency, and the last but not the least, S.A. Akinyemi Esq.

The Ondo Improvement League swept the polls in Ondo Division. There were two seats involved and its successful candidates were Chief F.O. Awosika and W.J. Falaiye, on whom I hope to comment subsequently.

The three Benin seats were won by Otu Edo candidates – Chiefs S.O. Ighodaro, H. Omo-Osagie and Chike Ekwuyasi – all of blessed memory. (please read more about these parties in Chapter 7).

Before the Lagos and Benin elections and in any case, towards the end of September 1951, the state of the parties was as follows:

Ondo Improvement League	2
Ibadan People's Party	6
NCNC/Independents	2
Action Group	39

The NCNC leaders, shocked and disappointed by the results of the elections launched a new wave of controversy and campaign against the genuineness of the results and this led Mr. Harold Cooper to cause to be published on the 29 September 1951 a statement absolving his department of blame for the controversy and disclosing further as follows:

(a) *that it was only the Action Group that submitted a list of its candidates to him for the final elections*

(b) *that no other lists were received although an official of Ibadan People's Party, in an interview with him (Mr. Cooper) identified the candidates of his party, and*

(c) *that of the winning candidates, the names of 38 were on the list sent to him by the Action Group.*

The full statement of Mr. Cooper, Public Relations Officer of the Nigerian Government, as published on the front page of *Daily Times* of Saturday 29 September 1951 is hereunder quoted in full.

It was captioned "Only Action Group men can be identified, PRO" and it reads:

"At a press conference held some days before the elections and at which all the three Lagos dailies were represented, it was agreed that I should write to the main parties and ask them to send me a list of their candidates, so that it would be possible, in announcing the results to say on which list each candidate's name occurred. (If a name had occurred on more than one list, this also would have been mentioned).

The headquarters of the Action Group sent me such list. It was the same as the list published in two of the Lagos dailies on the morning of the election.

No other lists were received.

Although an official of the Ibadan people's Party, in an interview with me, identified the candidates which he said represented his party.

We were thus left with no means of identifying the candidates of the other parties concerned and, since this made it impossible to give a complete picture of what was happening in terms of party affiliation, we decided to announce only the names.

Of the winning candidates, the names of 38 were on the list sent to me by the Action Group.

The six successful candidates at Ibadan were all among those who had been identified to me as representing the Ibadan People's Party.

No claim of any kind had reached us about the party affiliation of the remaining successful candidates.

Now that the election is over, there is still dispute about the party allegiance of many of the winning candidates. The official view is that each of these candidates has the right to reveal his party affiliation or to conceal it, according to his preference, and that it would not be proper for him to be questioned on the subject by a government officer.

Those candidates who wish to make their allegiance clear beyond cavil have an opportunity to do so through their party organizations or by sending statements direct to the press.

The aim of the Public Relations Department through-out the elections has been to maintain an attitude of complete neutrality but at the same time to do everything possible to report the results in terms of political parties in cases where the line between the contending parties were clearly drawn by the parties themselves."

That was the statement of Mr. Cooper, the Government Public Relations Officer who cleverly gave kudos to those who should have them and blame for those who caused the confusion generated by the claims and counter-claims of 1951 Parliamentary elections in the West.

4

Proofs of AG's victory

Publication of loyalty pacts by AG

IN ORDER TO convince all Nigerians and the world that it has won a well-deserved victory, the Action Group decided to take a number of steps. As a prelude to these steps, it came out with a statement on 5 October 1951, promising to bring all its successful candidates for presentation to Nigerians, in Lagos, at a public rally.

While the preparation for the rally was going on, the party got most of its legislators to sign pacts of loyalty and the list of those who signed was published in the press on Thursday 11 October 1951. A statement issued along with the pacts of loyalty by the party and published in the *Daily Times* of the same day, reads as follows:

"The list of candidates released before the general elections into the Western House of Assembly shows that 38 candidates of the Action group were successful at the polls and gave the party an easy lead over all other parties and Independents put together.

In order to avoid confusion and to establish the majority of the Action Group, once for all, to the satisfaction of the Nigerian public, the Action Group publishes today the declaration of 39 members of the Western House of Assembly who were at the time of election, members of the Action Group.

By this declaration each of the 39 members excepting two now in the United Kingdom, reaffirmed his loyalty to the Action Group, pledged support and subjected himself to the discipline of the party.

The two members of the Action Group to whom reference is made in the last paragraph are Rev. Banjo and Mr. Odebiyi. The fact that these two gentlemen are members of the Action

Group is not in dispute as this has been admitted in several publications in the "West African Pilot".

Not taking into consideration the large number of successful Independent candidates who have now signified their intention of becoming members of the Action Group, the position now is that the Action Group has a majority of six over the Independents, the NCNC and the IPP combined.

At the conference which opens with the triumphant entry and procession in Lagos on the 19th of October 1951, the successful members of the Action Group together with the Independent members, who would by then have become members, will appear before the public and make personal declarations.

The Action Group having given such clear proof of its majority will no longer be prepared to go into further controversy on this issue. "As the party with the majority in the House, the Action Group must concentrate its organizational machinery on increasing its majority by winning the Lagos and Benin elections and must then settle down to evolving plans whereby it can vigorously pursue its program for 'Freedom for all and life more abundant.'

The above quoted statement and the declaration referred to therein were published on pages 1 and 6 respectively, of the *Daily Times* of Thursday 11 October 1951.

Before I conclude my comments on the AG pacts of loyalty, may I throw some more light on the document. The first is that the name of Chief J.A.O. Odebiyi and Rev. S.A. Banjo, who were away in the UK got included, on trust, and it is on record that they did justify the confidence reposed in them by the party. Chief Odebiyi, in particular, is still very much around keeping the Awolowo political flag flying.

Readers will also observe that names and signatures of three other legislators – Alhaji D.S. Adegbenro, Messrs J.O. Oshuntokun and S.O. Hassan appear in the pacts. These gentlemen from Egba, Ekiti and Epe divisions, respectively, were, no doubt, AG scribes whose electoral influence was underestimated in their divisions, hence their inability to have their names included in the official list of candidates released by the party prior to the elections. They contested and won and they were, on request, accepted back into the fold.

The names of two other Assemblymen – R.A. Olusa of Owo Division and C. Tewe of Okitipupa, both of whom won on AG ticket, are missing in the pacts of loyalty. This is because the gentlemen could not be reached to sign and the party would not delay publication beyond their scheduled date. If these two legislators had appended their signatures to the pacts, the AG number of legislators would have been 41, instead of 39 as published. As expected, the two gentlemen subsequently fell in line with their colleagues.

The last point I like to make is that the pacts of loyalty prove conclusively that the five IPP members did not join the Action group until after 11 October 1951 – the day of the publication of the pacts. If they had joined on or before that date, their names and signatures would have been included in the document.

The Action Group having released the list of its candidates prior to the elections, having established its majority, traceable to its list of candidates, and having indicated its intention to present all its successful candidates to Nigerians in Lagos between 19 and 21 October and having also got those successful candidates to sign pacts of loyalty which had been published in the press, thought it had done enough to silence its opponent. It was mistaken.

NCNC reaction to the loyalty pacts

A day after the publication of the pacts of loyalty, the NCNC reacted in a way to ridicule the AG publication. The party in a statement published in the *West African Pilot* described the AG's declaration as "a parade of signatures and a ruse". It also asserted that the declaration, "established nothing but hysteria and feeling of uncertainty". It ended by appealing to NCNC members and supporters "to wait until the House meets before we demonstrate our majority"

They never did and could not have done.

Presentation of Assemblymen in Lagos

As earlier promised, the Action Group took its second major step by bringing all its legislators to Lagos. It was a triumphant entry into the city followed by a conference and a big rally during the course of which the party's Assemblymen numbering 41 as at that date, were presented to Nigerians in Lagos.

It must be pointed out that but for the courage, dogged determination, loyalty and commitment of the AG legislators, their arrival in Lagos would have been aborted. This was because the NCNC had organized their supporters to boo, heckle and disrupt the AG procession along their route especially from Ikeja to the Mainland of Lagos. It was when the procession of the envoys got to Iddo and Idunmota along the old Carter Bridge that they fell into the waiting hands of the enthusiastic supporters who welcomed them very warmly.

There were 165 cars in the legislators' procession which paid homage to Oba Adeniji Adele II of Lagos at the Iga Idunganran, the Oba's palace, and also visited the residences of Dr. Akinola Maja and Sir. Adeyemo Alakija, before retiring for the day.

The Assemblymen at Onikan Stadium and Island Club, Lagos

The Action Group took the third step to demonstrate its majority on Saturday 21 October 1951, at King George V Stadium, now known as Onikan Stadium, which was the venue of an international soccer competition between Nigeria and Ghana (then Gold Coast) for the Jalco Cup. The party brought all its legislators to the stadium and arrangements were made for them to sit together to watch the match. They were seated at the Island Club end of the field between the goal posts and the players' dressing rooms. This area is now opposite the VIP section of Onikan Stadium. The special spectators interacted with the other spectators and answered many of their questions during the half-time and at the end of the match. The day was a joyful one especially when the annual soccer encounter resulted in a 5-0 victory for Nigeria.

Dr. Azikiwe and Chief Awolowo were in the stadium to watch the Nigeria/Ghana soccer match as special guests. This, in addition to the presence of the AG Assemblymen naturally attracted media attention. The *Daily Times*, to quote one example, in its issue of Monday 22 October 1951, reported as follows:

"On Saturday, Action Group members of the House of Assembly attended the international match between Gold-Coast and Nigeria. A section of the football fans cheered Mr. Obafemi Awolowo, president of the Action Group, while another section hailed Zeek Zeek as Dr. Nnamdi Azikiwe, national president of the National Council of Nigeria and the Cameroons, entered the football ground."

Later that evening, the AG legislators were guests at the Island Club, Lagos, where they made themselves available for discussions and questioning by members of the club. That was the fourth step by AG to prove its majority.

Earlier, on Saturday 20 October 1951, the envoys and executive members of the AG met at Dr. Maja's old Bar Beach house at 9.00am to discuss the following:

(1) Rules governing the establishment of parliamentary councils and committees etc;
(2) Principles governing the appointment of ministers and selection of the members of the House of Representatives;
(3) Federal unity of Nigeria and meeting with Leaders of Thought of Northern and Eastern Regions,
(4) Self-government for Nigeria.

On Sunday 21 October 1951, the big rally of the party was held at the old Glover Memorial Hall, Marina, Lagos. According to a report on the front page of the *Daily Times* of Tuesday 23 October 1951, there were over 2,000 people in the hall with over 8,000 outside it and by the time the rally was over, the crowd had been joined by over 2,000 onlookers. The *Daily Times* of the same day and of the same page reported the rally further as follows:

Chief Bode Thomas, Balogun of Oyo and Secretary of the Group, during a speech as the meeting said that the Group had increased its majority by two over its previous number of 39 in the Western House of Assembly. Four more independent members have signified their intention to become members of the Group, so that "our majority", the Chief told meeting, "will be increased by another four." With 45 people declaring for the Group, the Chief said, he could not reconcile NCNC hopes for a majority with reality. He said it was apparent that the leader of the NCNC wanted to confuse issues.

Greeted with cheers, Chief Thomas asked certain candidates whom he said were being claimed by the NCNC to declare their stand publicly. Each of these men reaffirmed his loyalty to the Action Group.

Dr. Akinola Maja was the chairman of the rally which was also addressed, among others, by Chief Enahoro.

Earlier at the rally, Chief Awolowo had announced the five AG candidates for the Lagos elections. They were Dr. Maja, Alhaji Jubril Martin, Chief F.R.A. Williams, Chief M.A. Ogun and N.A.B. Kotoye Esq.

NCNC reaction to AG's proofs

While the Action group was doing everything possible to prove its majority, the NCNC continued to generate controversy but by now in a weak form.

Its latest reaction was a statement issued by its Central Working Committee through its National Secretary, Chief Kola Balogun.

The statement published in the *Daily Times* of 23 October 1951 reads in full:

"The Central working Committee reassures the general public and NCNC ardent supporters that the claim of the Action Group to be able to send 34 Groupers from the Western House to the House of Representatives is totally unfounded in view of the act that every division in the West is entitled to at least one seat in the House of Representatives and large divisions like Lagos, Ibadan, Urhobo are likely to have at least two seats in the House of Representatives. It is obvious that in a number of divisions, NCNC has a clear majority.

As the NCNC has stated again and again, control in the Western House in this matter of election of members to House of Representatives, as in many other matters, will be clear only when business begins in the Western House. Then there shall be great surprises for the Action Group and their minions. Let NCNC supporters be of good cheer, the position is well in hand."

Meanwhile, the campaign for the Lagos election was hotting up and Dr. Azikiwe in one of his speeches declared on November 16 that he and his colleagues would not accept ministerial appointments after the elections. Intelligent political observers and analysts linked this speech with Zik's overall failure in the Western elections. On the other hand, the Action Group Parliamentary Council met on 1 December 1951 and decided to sponsor only members of the party for ministerial posts.

AG legislators' letters to the Chief Commissioner

On 6 December 1951, the Action Group took the fifth step to demonstrate its majority.

Letters written and signed by all its elected members affirming their membership of and loyalty to the AG party were forwarded to the then Chief Commissioner and later Governor of the West, Sir Chandos Hoskyns-Abrahall.

Zik's call for coalition

On Friday 14 December 1951, Zik came out with what many people regarded as a bombshell.

It was an open letter to Chief Awolowo, leader of the Action Group, suggesting a coalition government in the West. The letter was widely reported in the press.

As a matter of fact, it attracted the headline of the *Daily Times* of Saturday 15 December 1951. In support of his call for cooperation and coalition in the West, Dr. Azikiwe was quoted as saying:

"We of the NCNC can count on a surprisingly commanding number of members in the Western House of Assembly; with your equally large number of members, the two parties can present a united front and create such a deadlock in the Western provinces as to force the hands of Government to concede to us a better Constitution whose provisions would make party politics more effective."

Dr. Azikiwe went on to say that even though the two parties had fundamental differences, *"we all favor Federation of Nigeria, universal adult suffrage, cabinet ministry according to accepted international practice and self-government".*

He assured Awo that he harbored no personal feeling against him and his party; on the contrary, he said *"I have criticized you without any ulterior motive*". Dr. Azikiwe's letter to Awo ends thus:

"In a colonial territory, it is not enough for one party to hold a slim majority in a Regional legislature and to exercise a measure of influence over its executives; what historians and political scientists will decide is whether in doing so, fundamental issues were compromised so as to pose the guilty ones to righteous indignation and condemnation."

This open letter from Dr. Azikiwe did not concede victory to Awo but it went near doing so. As for the call for a coalition in the West which was the main theme of Zik's open letter, I must point out that Awo could not persuade his party colleagues to change their decision of 1 December 1951. This was to sponsor only AG members for cabinet posts.

5

Final Proof of AG's majority

THE CONTROVERSY AS regards majority party was still on and the Action Group decided to give the sixth and final proof of its majority and this time on the floor of the House.

Before the meeting of the House of Assembly, the party came out with a statement reported on 5 January 1952 to the effect that it would insist on seats in the House being arranged on party basis in order to show which party was the majority.

The first session of Western Parliament took place at Agodi, Ibadan, on the 7, 8 and 10 January 1952.

On the first day of the session, the Action Group members set out from Chief Awolowo's Ibadan residence and were led in procession by Awo and Bode Thomas. They all wore AG party badges on their robes.

On entering the hall and discovering that the NCNC Assemblymen who had arrived earlier did not sit together but scattered themselves all over the Chamber, the AG leaders refused to take their seats.

Their leader Awo called them out and demanded that seats in the House be arranged on party basis and in his words, *"in a separate, distinct and identifiable manner"*. His party was determined to put an end to the confusion arising from claims and counter claims as to the majority party in the House. His was the majority party and he was bent on demonstrating it inside the House.

The NCNC which had in the past appealed to its supporters to wait for the meeting of the House to see them demonstrate their majority developed cold feet! They sat tight!

The Assembly officials in worried postures appealed for compromise from the two sides, but this failed. They then shifted their appeal to the eminent Obas of those days, notably Sir Adesoji Aderemi, the Ooni of Ife, Sir Ladapo Ademola, the Alake of Abeokuta, Oba Akenzua of Benin and Oba Samuel Akinsanya, the Odemo of Isara, for help.

The traditional fathers felt Awo's demand was reasonable. Speaking on behalf of himself and all his colleagues, the Alake of Abeokuta, Sir Ladapo Ademola told the British officials who wanted to get them to persuade Awo and his men to change their stand not to waste their time. *"They are not coming in and we are with them,"* emphasized the Alake.

After this demonstration of strength, the demand of Awo and his Assemblymen was granted. The seats were rearranged on party basis. Awo and his team reentered the hall amidst a loud ovation from the Obas, chiefs and distinguished spectators in the gallery.

The first day of the first session of the Western House was widely reported by most newspapers in the country. The *Daily Times* of Tuesday 8 January 1952, on page 12, reported as follows:

"Action Group majority in the Western House of Assembly was publicly exhibited and officially acknowledged at the first meeting of the Western Regional Legislature held here this morning.

Forty nine of them with badges pinned on their dresses waited outside the hall and posed for photograph.

They insisted on sitting together as a party and the Civil Secretary, Western Region, granted their request.

Loud cheers from the hall and from hundreds of supporters outside greeted them as they entered the hall led by Mr. Obafemi Awolowo, leader of the party. They looked unassuming but they are the men who will wield political power in Western Nigeria for the next five years. Members of the House of Chiefs sat on one side of the House.

Forty-nine Action Group members of the Assembly sat as a block on another side, while NCNC and Independent candidates sat together."

Thus the Action Group gave another and final proof of its majority and this time in Parliament.

There were carpet-crossings afterwards during and after the life of that Parliament to and from all the parties, not only in the West but also in the East, the North and at the National level.

However, there is no doubt that the Action Group of Nigeria won the Western elections of 1951, beating the NCNC hands down.

6

Zik and the HOR seat--his failure to win a seat in the House of Representatives

In accordance with the Constitution of the day, election of members of the House of Representatives from the West was done according to the specified number of seats for each of the 25 divisions of the Region. In a division where the number of contestants was not more the number of seats allocated to that division, there would be no need to ballot among the 80 legislators in the House in respect of that division, but if otherwise, the necessity for a ballot would arise.

Lagos had five members in the House of Assembly, two of whom were to go to the House of Representatives. The NCNC having won all the five seats in Lagos ought to have no problem in getting two of their five members to the Centre. All they needed to do was to meet and decide which two of their five would go and thereby avoid the House choosing for them by ballot. However, they had a big problem in choosing the two!

On 28 November 1951 the *Daily Times* came out with the report that the NCNC party and its allies could not agree among themselves as to which two candidates would represent Lagos in the House of Representatives. Majority of the NCNC members favored Zik and Adedoyin while members of the NNDP (Demos) almost without exception wanted Zik and Olorun-Nimbe. Those who supported Prince Adedoyin took into consideration his great commitment to the cause of the party especially his sacrifice in respect of Adele-Oyekan tussle for the stool of Oba of Lagos. He was the chief propagandist of the NCNC and its allies and he contributed not a little to their electoral victories.

Dr. Abubakar Ibiyinka Olorun-Nimbe on the other hand, was a class by himself: honest, politically reliable, dignified in appearance, brilliant and with a wonderful command of the English language. Dr. Olorun-Nimbe was highly courageous and once he took a stand on an issue, it was most difficult, if not impossible, to move him.

Before their election on 20 November 1951, he, Dr. Olorun-Nimbe, had indicated that if elected, he would make his services available at the Centre. This desire of his was considered legitimate and solidly backed by NNDP members and the Market Women Associations. The fact that he was the first Mayor of Lagos reinforced their stand.

The NCNC, it will be recalled came to life in 1945, like the National Democratic Coalition (NADECO) of today, as a coalition of organizations rather than of individuals.

The first president of NCNC, Mr. Herbert Macaulay, was the founder and president of the Nigerian National Democratic Party (NNDP).

In the two major elections contested and decisively won by the NCNC in Lagos between 1950 and 1951, (municipal and parliamentary), the party had operated as a grand alliance of NCNC/NNDP/Market-Women/Labor.

For example, in selecting their candidates for the 1951 elections, they were careful to include a labor representative, H.P. Adebola, while Dr. Olorun-Nimbe was more a candidate of the NNDP and the Market Women within the group than of the others.

In supporting Olorun-Nimbe's ambition for a seat in the National Parliament, his admirers placed premium on:

(i) his strength of character;

(ii) his longer and richer experience as a councilor of the Lagos Town Council and a legislator in the old Legislative Council;

(iii) his scoring the highest popular vote in the election to the Western House of Assembly held on 20 November 1951;

(iv) and on the sentimental but strong point that he was the only indigenous Lagosian among the elected five Lagos Assemblymen.

By the 5th of January 1952, the great headache was still with the NCNC. As a matter of fact on that day supporters of Prince Adedoyin walked out of an NNDP reconciliation meeting. The signs were ominous.

On 7 January 1952, when members of the House of Assembly met and those interested in House of Representatives election were invited to indicate, Zik, Nimbe and Adedoyin got up to put their names down for election. Later, T.O.S. Benson and H.P. Adebola too submitted their names for election. All these happened, as hinted above, on Monday 7th January 1952 and as the election was billed for the following Thursday, many party supporters and admirers felt that last minute efforts to resolve the big crisis would be made.

When the House of Assembly met on Thursday 10th January 1952, all the five NCNC members for Lagos were still listed to contest the House of Representatives election! None had withdrawn! The election took place on that same day as scheduled, and the results were as follows:

Adedoyin	...	67
Olorun-Nimbe	...	51
Azikiwe	...	27
Adebola	...	1
Benson	...	Nil

Adedoyin and Olorun-Nimbe were, therefore, elected.

Later in the day and as a result of massive and emotional appeals by NCNC leaders, many of whom were weeping profusely at their meeting, over what they felt was "the calamity which had occurred that day to the party and the

Nation, nay to Africa", Adedoyin "decided" to resign as a member of House of Representatives. He signed the letter of resignation which was sent by registered post by the NCNC secretariat to the president of the House of Representatives.
But less than 24 hours after sending the letter of resignation, he sent another withdrawing it. Explaining this latest and curious move, the *Daily Times* on the front page of its issue of 12th January 1952 quoted Prince Adedoyin of accusing his party of tribal animosity and of conspiracy against him. He was also quoted as saying that but for the Action Group members who voted massively for him, he would have scored only 10 votes. He believed he was regarded within the NCNC as a camp follower. Prince Adedoyin also revealed that in the absence of Zik at the Centre, a plan had been hatched by his party colleagues outside Yorubaland to make Professor Eyo Ita the NCNC leader in the House of Representatives and he (Adedoyin) the deputy, whereas the Professor, to quote his words, "is by far my junior in the NCNC." He ended his interview with the *Daily Times* by affirming that he was not a fool and added, "a fool at 40 is a fool forever".
The above stated account paints the picture of how and why Dr. Azikiwe did not make it to the House of Representatives in 1952. The cause was more of indiscipline within his NCNC than anything else.
Dr. Olorun-Nimbe was punished. He was expelled from the NCNC. The NNDP, however, did not see anything wrong with what he did. To the best of my knowledge, nothing happened to Prince Adedoyin. He went scot-free. He was able to argue quite successfully that he was a candidate of all the groups within the alliance – NCNC/NNDP/Market-Women/Labor.
Before bringing this chapter to an end, it is necessary to comment on a few points, some of them well-meaning that have been canvassed. Some people have asked, for example, why did the AG not show magnanimity and vote Zik to the

House of Representatives? This could raise another question. Why did the great Zik with his NCNC who had lost a well-contested electoral battle not demonstrate magnanimity and spirit of sportsmanship by conceding victory to his opponent who won? Why were they using all sorts of tricks including scattered sitting arrangement in the House, on the day of the first session of parliament, on 7 January 1952? If the AG legislators had voted for him, would that not add to the confusion already generated by NCNC as regards the majority party in the House of Assembly?

The NCNC leaders were never tired of flogging the issue of Zik's defeat on the floor of House of Assembly in January 1952. They should ask themselves why have the AG leaders not been flogging all the political crimes they of the NCNC committed against them between 1962 and 1963? Did the NCNC legislators not join hands with NPC to set aside in the Federal Parliament the Privy Council judgment that declared Alhaji Adegbenro the rightful and legitimate Premier of Western Nigeria? They did. Furthermore, did they not join hands with Chief Akintola's NNDP to topple AG's Government in the West? The AG leaders had not flogged these issues in the interest of unity and understanding.

Some NCNC leaders and supporters had attributed Dr. Azikiwe's defeat in the 1952 elections in Ibadan to House of Representatives to ethnicity. This is unfortunate. This group of people ought to be reminded that when Zik returned to Nigeria from Ghana in 1937, he, after careful consideration, decided to settle in Lagos which was and still is predominantly Yoruba. He got on very well among them socially, commercially and more importantly, politically. He and his party won many electoral victories. This was regarded as normal but when his political opponents decided not to vote for him on the floor of the House of Assembly, they read ethnic motive into the action. The issue, of course, was political.

Let me conclude this chapter by comparing Zik's case with that of his party colleague, Dr. O. Ajibade. He was a Yoruba private medical practitioner who settled and made Port Harcourt his home in 1939. He interacted very well with the generality of the people and thus became the president of Port Harcourt Community League. Dr. Ajibade was interested in politics and was one of the foundation members of the NCNC in Port Harcourt which was by 1951, an Igbo town, population wise and an NCNC stronghold. The well-known and colorful Barrister A.C. Nwapa and Dr. Ajibade were the chairman and vice-chairman, respectively, of the local branch of the NCNC. The two gentlemen applied to contest the 1951 election on the platform of their beloved party and both were nominated by its nomination committee.

Soon after, a new committee was set up by the party to look again into the nomination issue and the new committee decided, for reasons not clear to many, to drop Dr. Ajibade's name for that of the one and only chief M.C.K. Ajuluchukwu! Meanwhile, more NCNC leaders, namely Councilor R.O. Madueme, Z.C. Obi, V.K. Onyeri and G.C. Nonyelu decided to join the electoral battle as contestants. The National Secretariat of the NCNC, embarrassed at the turn of events decided to intervene. According to *the Daily Times* of Thursday 15 November 1951, the party directed from Lagos on November 14 that the nomination of Barrister A.C. Nwapa and Dr. O. Ajibade should stand. Many people shouted hurrah!

That however, was not the end of the story. The combatants were already geared for action. As a matter of fact, all the NCNC independent candidates went ahead to contest. None withdrew. The election took place on Tuesday 27 November

1951 A.C. Nwapa won, while his able and loyal vice-chairman Ajibade was defeated by his own party men!

The detailed results were as follows:

A.C. Nwapa	35
V.K. ONyeri	33
Z.C. Obi	28
G.C. Nonyelu	27
M.C.K. Ajuluchukwu	24
R.O. Madueme	20
Dr. O. Ajibade	12

Taking into consideration all the facts about his nomination and subsequent defeat, it is difficult to rule out the possibility of ethnic bias in the case of Ajibade. His defeat, in any case, was a big blow to the slogan of "One country one destiny" and the "policy of creating a political climate healthy enough to make one a citizen of wherever he lived", which Dr. Mbadiwe trumpeted in his book, *"Rebirth of a Nation"*. Lastly, Ajibade's defeat robbed us of an opportunity of being able to have a Westerner as an elected member of the Eastern House of Assembly as we could name many Easterners who were elected legislators on the Western side of our great country.

7

Political Alignments-- of Divisional Organizations.

Throughout the period of the Western Nigeria elections and after, the NCNC gave the impression and in fact made the claims that all the local or divisional parties that did well in the elections were its allies. For example, it did lay claim to the support of members of Ibadan People's Party (IPP), Ondo Improvement League and Otu Edo of Benin.

I will very much like to assert that many of the local parties were independent and were interested in being on the winning side. They were very careful not to antagonize any of the two main parties. They maintained lines of communication with them.

Below are profiles of some of the parties:

Ibadan People's Party (IPP)

This was a party formed in Ibadan by a group of young and middle-aged Ibadan citizens. It was out to engage in political battle with the Ibadan Citizen's Council (ICC) in Ibadan division. The primary objective was to gain the upper hand in Ibadan politics by winning the 1951 elections. And this they achieved admirably. The leaders of the IPP were A.M.A. Akinloye (president), Adegoke Adelabu (vice-president), Moyosore Aboderin, a financial pillar of the organization, Chief D.T Akinbiyi, who later became the Olubadan of Ibadan and S.O. Lanlehin, who was a big wig in the ruling Action Group. There was also S.A. Akinyemi, a retired police officer.

All these gentlemen contested the 1951 elections and won. As regards their commitment to either of the two parties, it was very clear that they were not in alliance with either of the two as a group. On individual basis, however, some of them were. For instance, Adegoke Adelabu who later grew up to become a political octopus, was an NCNC disciple, while Moyosore Aboderin and D.T. Akinbiyi were on the Action Group side.

In order to drive home the point that the IPP was not firmly committed to any of the big parties, it is important to refer to a few incidents. By 25 June 1951, the Nigerian People's Congress, led by Chief HO Davies, published a list of officers and other members of its national executive in the press. It was a formidable and inspiring list including, apart from the colossus, H.O.D. himself, as leader and president, such stalwarts as Dr. C. Anozie, Messrs M.O. Bakare, Adewale Thompson, T.E.O. Roberts, Charles Nwanaka and C.O. Ogunbanjo. Others were Fagbenro Beyioku, J.M. Udochi, R.S.S. Coker, P.J. Oshoba, Ajani Olujare and the one and only T.A.B. Oki, etc.

The IPP, believing as many other political analysis did that H.O.D's Nigerian People's Congress would make a great impact on the results of 1951 Western elections, sent a delegation to Lagos

to meet H.O. Davies and his members with a view to striking a working accord with them. The delegates, after their useful meeting, were entertained to dinner at the old Savoy Hotel by Mrs. H.O. Davies.

The IPP, it will be recalled, had earlier on agreed to "cooperate" with the NCNC.

All these developments which took place before the elections, were reported in the press, particularly the *Daily Times.* Chief Obafemi Awolowo too, recorded the IPP delegation's meetings with Chiefs Davies and Akintola in his 1951 *Political Diary* on 24 August 1951.

The final election in Ibadan as well as most of the other parts of the West took place on 24 September 1951. The IPP, as stated earlier, won all the six seats at stake. About two weeks after this victory was confirmed, Chief Kola Balogun, the National Secretary of the NCNC sent declaration forms to the elected IPP assembly men urging them to declare their support for the NCNC. The IPP leader, Chief Akinloye, returned all the forms unsigned.

Addressing a meeting of his party at Mapo Hall, Bere, in Ibadan where the decision to return the forms was made known, he, Akintoye, stated as follows:

"No independent party ever commits itself to another political organization"

He went further to remind his members that they agreed to "Cooperate" with the NCNC but not to "affiliate". He ended by also reminding them that they contested the election as independents.

Adegoke Adelabu, vice-chairman of the IPP, stoutly canvassed among members the need to pledge their loyalty to the NCNC since they had earlier agreed on "cooperation". He was opposed by many of his colleagues who described him as "an agent of Dr Azikiwe". Majority of the members felt it would be better to remain independent until the House of Assembly met.

The meeting subsequently took a decision to refer the matter to a committee of the party for consideration. Eventually, the IPP came out with a decision to align with the Action Group and so five of its six elected Assembly men joined the party while only Adegoke Adelabu went the NCNC way.

The Otu Edo of Benin

The Otu Edo was a divisional party that took the centre stage in Benin politics and was out to put at the back stage its local opponent – the Benin Tax-Payers Association, many of whose leaders were prominent members of the *Ogboni* society. The Otu Edo was a very popular organization backed by the Benin Monarch. Most of its leaders, on the Regional or National plane, were NCNC members or supporters. This, however, did not mean that all its leaders were in the NCNC. In November 1951, the NCNC came out officially with the names of its "candidates" for the 1951 elections in Benin. This was the second occasion they were doing so, the first time they did so officially and positively was in respect of Lagos election which took place about a week earlier – 20 November 1951. The three names released to the public were H. Omo-Osagie, S.O. Ighodaro and Chike Ekwuyasi, all well-known members of Otu Edo.

In publishing the names on the 29 November 1951, the *Daily Times* disclosed that "So far as it is known, Barrister S.O. Ighodaro counts leaders of the AG as among members of his own political school of thought".

"He had" continued the paper "Expressed it in close quarters that he is not a member of the NCNC". This did put some doubt on the NCNC list of three names and subsequent investigation proved that the three names were Otu Edo candidates which the NCNC tried to adopt.

As far as Barrister Ighodaro was concerned, there was no doubt that he was in the Action Group. This was known to close and unclose quarters. He was very active in building support for the party in Benin and was one of the brains behind the successful inauguration of the Benin provincial branch of the party, in Benin, on 4 April 1951. Officers were elected on the day as follows:

Mr D.N. Oronsaye - President
Barrister S.O. Ighodaro - Secretary
Mr J. Edomwoyi - Assist. Secretary
Mr Chike N. Ekwuyasi - Publicity Secretary

Although the last named officer above subsequently went to the NCNC, Barrister Ighodaro was with the Action Group – first, last, and all the time.

The full report of the Benin provincial conference of the Action Group at which Barrister Ighodaro was elected secretary, was published in *Daily Service* of 21 April 1951 Chief Ighodaro attended the Western Region historic conference of the AG in Owo and he was elected the Treasurer of the party. This too was reported in the dailies.

The Benin election took place on the 6 December 1951 and the three gentlemen won. Ighodaro scored the highest vote, Chief Omo-Osagie and Chike Ekwuyasi came second and third, respectively. As expected, Ighodaro went with AG while his other two colleagues joined forces with the NCNC.

Ondo Improvement League

The Ondo Improvement Leagues was the divisional organization on whose platform Messrs F.O. Awosika and W.J. Falaiye were elected. The names of the two gentlemen were not in the list of the Action Group candidates released before the final elections in September 1951. And as hinted earlier, the NCNC released no list of candidates in respect of the 72 seats contested in September 1951.

The Ondo Improvement League, like other nationalist/cultural organizations, had sympathy for the NCNC which was an umbrella body for most organizations in the early days of our struggles for independence. Mr. W.J. Falaiye was, business-wise, closer to the NCNC leadership as a newspaper agent and correspondent of the NCNC *West African Pilot* in Akure. Mr Falaiye's colleague, Chief F.O. Awosika was one of the most controversial legislators of the day. He was a very stately, respectable and knowledgeable man with a pre-possessing appearance. He was, before his election, neither a member of the NCNC nor of the Action Group, but his heart was more on the side of the latter.

In the book titled, *"Ayo Rosiji – Man with vision"*, published in 1992 and authored by an Australian, Nina E. Mba; a teacher at the University of Lagos, there was an interesting reference to Awosika. According to Nina Mba, it was Ayo Rosiji who won the heart of Awosika for the Action Group. Awosika, it would be recalled was Ayo Rosiji's teacher at Government College, Ibadan.

As reported in the book, it all happened just before the House of Assembly met in Ibadan in January 1952. A meeting of the NCNC leaders was taking place in the Methodist School Hall, Agbeni, Ibadan.

Dr. Nnamdi Azikiwe, the party leader, was addressing his members when Rosiji entered the hall and moved quietly to Awosika's seat in the front row and called him out under the very eyes of Zik and other members! While the two men were going out, Zik recognized Rosiji, signaled to his colleagues to stop them but they could not be stopped. They quickly got outside, entered Rosiji's car and sped away to his house in Ibadan where it took little persuasion to get Awosika to switch over to the Action Group.

The story ended by giving two reasons why it was easy to get Awosika to switch. The first was that his mind was not really with the NCNC and the second was that he recognized the strength of the Action Group in the House.

Some questions arise from this story. Why was it necessary for Rosiji to take the desperate and dramatic step of calling Awosika out of a meeting being addressed by such a political giant like Azikiwe in order to get him to change his allegiance? Could he not have reached his former secondary school teacher otherwise? Perhaps it is appropriate to refer to what Chief Awolowo had to say in his 1951 *Political Diary* on this issue I quote him as follows:

"November 21: In a letter published in the Pilot of this date, F.O. Awosika stated that he had been elected on the ticket of the Ondo Improvement League which had frowned on his declaration of support for the Action Group which he was now withdrawing. On 6/1/52, his friends including Canon Alayande pleaded with me and other Action Group leaders for his re-admission. It should be noted that Awosika was the Ondo Secretary of Egbe Omo Oduduwa since 1948, and though he stood for election on the platform of the Ondo Improvement

League of which he was an officer, there was a firm understanding by him to the leaders of the Egbe that he would declare for Action Group as soon as the election was over."

From all the above, it is clear that F.O. Awosika had declared for the Action Group before 21 November 1951 and since we were not told of the date Rosiji performed his "Wonders" at Methodist School, Agbeni, in Ibadan, we could not easily link Awosika's declaration with Rosiji's efforts. Furthermore, the Lagos election to the Western House of Assembly took place on November 20 and Dr Azikiwe and his party won all the five seats at stake. Was there any connection between Awosika's withdrawal of earlier declaration of support for the Action Group and NCNC victory in Lagos?

8

Azikiwe's reaction to Western Elections

IN 1970, ABOUT 20 years after the event, Dr Nnamdi Azikiwe reacted in black and white to the result of the election in his autobiography titled *"My Odyssey".*

He stated that the NCNC was under the 'impression' that it had won 43 seats out of 80 but 20 of the legislators whom they "regarded as members, supporters or sympathizers" aligned themselves with the Action Group. He listed these legislators, with reasons, as follows:

Chief Arthur Prest was legal adviser of NCNC in Sapele.

Chief Anthony Enahoro had been a supporter or sympathizer of the NCNC from time immemorial and the leadership of the party were of that opinion until after the election.

Chief W.J. Falaiye was NCNC representative at Akure and correspondent of the *"West Africa Pilot"* who was once selected by him (Zik) to fill a party position in Akure.

Chief F.O. Awosika was a candidate supported by NCNC Ondo branch.

Chief S. Akinola was a candidate supported by the NCNC Ilesa branch.

(6)-(10) Chief A.M.A. Akinloye was a candidate supported by the Mabolaje/NCNC Alliance at Ibadan.

Chiefs Aboderin, Akinbiyi and Lanlehin were also supported by the same alliance. Only Alhaji Adegoke Adelabu Joined the NCNC after the election.

(11) Chief S.Y. Kesington-Momoh was supported by the NCNC Afenmai or Kukuruku Division. He attended a caucus meeting of the Western House of Assembly in Ibadan. His colleague, Chief A.O. Ogedengbe was with the NCNC after the election and joined the AG later.

(12) Mr. Coker was supported by the NCNC in Iseyin. He entertained NCNC delegates in his house during the campaigns.

(13) Chief Bishop Fisher was supported by the NCNC at Badagry and he entertained NCNC delegates in his house during the electioneering campaign.

(14) Mr. R.A. Olusa was supported by the NCNC in Owo Division.

(15) Mr. J.G. Ako was supported by the Urhobo Progress Union and the NCNC in Urhobo Division.

(16) Mr. C.A. Tewe was supported by the NCNC in Okitipupa.

It is very important to comment on Dr. Azikiwe's reaction in respect of each of the above-named gentlemen and I respectfully state as follows:

Chief Arthur Prest

It may be true that Chief Prest was a legal adviser of the NCNC in Sapele, but that must be before he cut off his relationship with the NCNC to join the Action Group.

The Itsekiri Chief was one of the builders of the AG in Warri Province in particular and Midwest Region in general.

As early as 10 April 1951 when the Warri provincial Action Group was inaugurated, he was very much around with other pillars of the party to see Chief W.E. Mowarin and Barrister Mike Okorodudu elected chairman and secretary respectively.

A joint provincial conference of Benin and Warri Action Group took place in Sapele on 14 April 1951 and was attended by 33 delegates from the 12 districts of the two provinces.

Chiefs Arthur Prest and Anthony Enahoro were not only very much present, but they were also elected chairman and secretary, respectively. A full report of all these activities could be read in the *"Daily Service"* of 21 April 1951.

In addition to all the above, the inaugural conference of the Action Group in both Yoruba and Midwest Zones took place in Owo between 28 and 29 April 1951 and was hosted by Chief Ajasin.

At that historic conference, Chief Prest was elected one of the three vice-presidents of the Action Group and Chief Enahoro became an assistant secretary.

All these were published on and before the election in September 1951.

Chief Anthony Enahoro:

The great chief was one of those who made the Action Group what it was, and his membership of the party was not only from its root but also well-considered.

Chief Enahoro had met Awo, the leader of the party he later elected to join for the first time, on a fine afternoon in Awo's office for over an hour in Ibadan.

The two of them parted, after their meeting, with a favorable impression of each other. There was a meeting of minds on many political issues.

Early in 1951, the formation of the Action Group took place in Ibadan with many branches springing up in many parts of Yoruba land.

The organizers then sent emissaries to Benin, Sapele, Warri, etc. to contact the leaders in the areas including Chief Enahoro and invited them to form the Midwest Action Group which would emerge later to form the AG West, which in turn would form the nucleus of a nationwide political party.

Soon after, the Action Group in a publication explained that, among others, the purposes of the party were:

(i) To create an atmosphere in which the best available men, whatever the brand of their

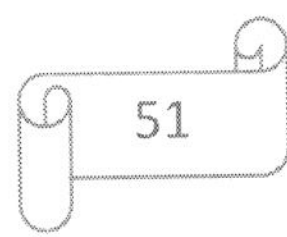

politics, could take an active part in shaping the nation's future.

(ii) To work for the introduction of a true Federal system in Nigeria.

(iii) To use the new Constitution to develop and modernize our educational and social services;

(iv) To declare, propagate, popularize and pursue a clear objective in regard to the question of self-government.

The first objective of the AG above was not to Chief Enahoro's liking, because it lacks ideological content, but he reasoned that it was better to have independence before talking of ideologies.

The last objective was very much to his liking and felt he must associate with a party to launch the final stage of the fight for independence. He believed his days of individual protest were over.

Chief Enahoro's desire received the enthusiastic support of his people especially the Uromi Improvement Union and Ishan Progress Union both of whom desired a number of amenities to which the Action Group manifesto had paid adequate attention.

The Ishan Progress Union, in particular had in fact taken advantage of Chief Enahoro's stay in Sapele, near their home, to establish close contact with the Chief and had invited him to represent Ishan Division in the legislature. The Chief's reason for associating with a political party had been strengthened.

The great nationalist could even have joined the NCNC which had enjoyed his sympathy and support in the past. After all, he had been in close contact with the leadership of that party. Why then did he decide not to join the NCNC? There were, of course, reasons for the decision. The first was that the NCNC was weak and inactive at that time. We hope to elaborate on this subsequently. Furthermore, Dr. Azikiwe, shortly before this time, had announced his retirement from politics for five years. This had confused many of his supporters.

In addition, relations between Chief Enahoro and many NCNC leaders had not been cordial since his 1949 imprisonment episode and these had not been improved by a critical pamphlet published by him on Dr. Azikiwe. Lastly, it was not clear to many people including Chief Enahoro whether the NCNC would continue to fight for self-government only outside or and also in parliament where the Uromi chief believed the next stage of the battle should largely shift.

In view of all the above, Chief Enahoro felt justified in accepting the invitation to convene a meeting of leaders of Benin and Warri Provinces which led to the formation of the Action Group in the Midwest. He was the General Secretary of the group in the zone.

The first joint conference of the Action Group was held at Owo on 28 and 29 April 1951 and was hosted by Chief Ajasin. It was attended y leaders from all over Yoruba land and the Milwest.

The conference proclaimed Awolowo as the president of the party, Arthur Prest as a vice-president and Bode Thomas as the General Secretary. Tony Enahoro was elected Assistant General Secretary.

There were two assistant secretaries and S.O. Shonibare was the other.

The happenings at Owo seemed to have jolted the NCNC as Chief Enahoro received a telegraphic invitation in Dr. Azikiwe's name inviting him to join the NCNC National Executive as an officer. The Uromi Chief replied that he was already committed.

The Action Group subsequently released for publication the list of its candidates for the 1951 Western election and the name of Anthony Enahoro was very much present on the list.

The election was held on 24 September 1951 and Anthony Eronsele Enahoro was elected first member for Ishan in the Western House of Assembly.

Chief W.J. Falaiye & Chief F.O. Awosika

We have already written on these two gentlemen in the preceding chapter seven.

Chief S. Akinola

He was supposed to have been supported by the Ilesa Branch of NCNC. Why was this necessary? Was he their candidate? The man claimed to be independent and joined the AG in the House.

Chiefs A.M.A. Akinloye, Moyo Aboderin, D.T. Akinbiyi, S.O. Lanlehin & Alhaji Adegoke Adelabu

These were five of the six men who won the election in Ibadan. The sixth was S.A. Akinyemi.

They all contested on Ibadan People's Party platform and defeated Ibadan Citizens Council's candidates. Please read our write-up on them in chapter seven.

The only thing we need to add here is that there was no Mabolaje-NCNC Alliance in Ibadan in 1951 when the election took place. Alhaji Adelabu formed his Mabolaje Grand Alliance in 1953 following a law enacted in November 1953 by the Action Group Government which removed illiterate judges from the presidency of customary courts and also banned touts from such premises .

Adelabu regarded this as a slap in the traditional institution and formed Mabolaje/NCNC Grand Alliance to fight the cause of the displaced chiefs most of whom gave their support to him and his organization.

We like to end this comment on Ibadan legislators by quoting from an interview the late Chief Moyo Aboderin gave to the *Sunday Punch* of 20 October 1985.

According to the chief, "Dr. Azikiwe had sent telegrams to all the six elected members of Ibadan People's Party urging them to join his party, the NCNC". "His strategy", he said "was however faulty since he relied mostly on Adelabu and Akinloye and thought that by getting the two of them he would be able to switch the other members to his camp".

The chief stated further: "I favored the Action Group and I succeeded in getting all the members with the exception of Adelabu to the AG".

In the same interview, Chief Aboderin who in the elections to the House of Assembly scored 82 votes to Akinloye's and Adelabu's 81 and 61, respectively, asserted: "The popular idea that the IPP cross-carpeted from the NCNC to the Action Group is therefore, erroneous"

Chief S.Y. Kesington-Momoh

This legislator, as far as the Action Group was concerned, was an NCNC man and he was regarded as such by all.

On 10 January 1952, he and two others, namely, J.G. Ako and Awodi Orisaremi, from Urhobo and Kukuruku divisions, crossed to the Action Group.

The three of them were convinced that the AG was the majority party and wanted their votes for the House of Representatives election billed for the day.

In his 1951/52 *Political Diary*, Chief Awolowo recorded the event as follows:

"On the floor f the House of Assembly, S.Y .Kesington-Momoh crossed carpet from the NCNC to the AG; so did J.G .Ako and Awodi Orisaremi.

They all wanted Action Group votes to enable them to get elected to the House of Representatives.

After a considerable amount of importunities commencing from the afternoon of 7/1/52 to the evening of 8/1/52, the AG Parliamentary Council agreed to admit them to the membership of the party provided – (1) they paid £5 each for enrolment (1/- was enrolment fee); (2) made generous contributions to the party's fund and (3) were prepared to demonstrate their change of party allegiance on the floor of the House of Assembly.

In the result, however, only Kesington-Momoh and J.G. Ako were elected to the House of Representatives to represent Kukuruku and Urhobo Divisions, respectively, which had only one member Each in the House. Soon afterwards, Awodi Orisaremi re-ratted to the NCNC."

Mr. Coker of Iseyin

Iseyin was and is still part of Oyo Division and there was no Coker among the Oyo legislators of those days.

There were five of them elected in 1951: their names were Bode Thomas, Abiodun Akerele, A.B.P. Martins, T.A. Amao and S.B. Eyitayo.

We do not know how the NCNC leader came about Coker whom they voted for and who entertained them in Iseyin during the campaigns in 1951.

Rev. G.M. Fisher & R.A. Olusa

The names of the two gentlemen were on the list of the Action Group candidates for Badagry and Owo Divisions, respectively.

The list was made public before the final elections on 24 September 1951. If in spite of this the NCNC decided to support them, it is they who should explain why.

J.G. Ako

Mr. Ako as explained above was one of the legislators who openly declared for the Action Group in the House of Assembly on 10 January 1952.

This was not the first association of Mr. Ako with the Action Groupers as he and many other prominent leaders in the Midwest attended and addressed the joint provincial conference of Benin and Warri Action Group which was held in Sapele in April 1951.

The others, who like him addressed the conference were Chiefs Arthur Prest, Tony Enahoro, S.Y. Eke, Chike Ekwuyasi and Festus Edah who later became Festus Okotie-Eboh and many others who jointly resolved to form the Midwest zones of the Action Group.

This was fully reported on the front page of the *Daily Service* of 21 April 1951.

C.A. Tewe

Mr. Tewe was an Action Group candidate as the official party list would show. Why then did the NCNC support him as claimed by their leader?

9

Why the Action Group won

THE FOREGOING ACCOUNT no doubt goes to prove that the Action Group won the 1951 parliamentary election in the West and that the NCNC lost. Why was this so? There were many reasons for this state of affairs.

By the year 1951, the NCNC had tremendous goodwill but lacked organization. One of the reasons for this was the proscription on 13 April 1950, of the Zikist Movement. This organization was the militant and most effective wing of the NCNC. In an *Extraordinary Gazette* which announced its proscription, it was declared an unlawful society under section 62 of the Criminal Code.

Its aims were pronounced seditious and its means and methods adjudged lawless and violent. The suffering of these patriots were, no doubt, painful but more painful was the lack of understanding and appreciation by the NCNC leadership.

As a matter of fact, the Zikists were denounced and this shattered and disorganized them. Consequently, the Zikists did not participate in the election of 1951 as they would have if they had been in the correct form; and this affected the results in favor of the Action Group.

It is also important to note that at that time the official stand of the NCNC was to boycott the Macpherson Constitution and the legislature, in favor of 'positive action'.

This must have influenced the Zikist Movement to have prepared such a seditious document as the "Program of work, 1950-51", which recommend such measures, among others, as intensive boycott and anti-tax campaign; public assemblies and demonstrations in contravention of public orders; flying of "black flags" before so-called imperialist agents and stooges and also displaying of revolutionary slogans, posters, caricatures and proclamations in streets, houses, offices, schools, workshops, etc.

This was the immediate cause of the Zikist Movement's trouble with the authorities.

Earlier, Dr. Azikiwe had announced a five-year retirement or ban from politics on himself, because he was not prepared to "impose himself on a people unready for action"

And when members of the Zikist Movement were being jailed for "action", their national leader made a public pronouncement about youthful impetuosity.

Many of the compatriots knew the statement was directed at them and their pain and disappointment could better be imagined! Some of them wept bitterly and openly!

In spite of these happenings which had made the NCNC less active and without much organization on the ground, the party still enjoyed tremendous popular sentiment and this made their leadership to be over-confident.

At a meeting of his party at the Glover Memorial Hall in September 1951, Dr. Azikiwe, the leader, claimed that the NCNC would win 50 to 60 seats in the pending Western elections.

This was reported in the *Daily Times* of 20 September 1951. Incidentally, Chief Awolowo noted this in his 1951 *Political Dairy.*

There were at that time internal squabbles and indiscipline within the NCNC. The best example of these was the event which led to all the five NCNC legislators contesting among themselves for the two seats allocated to Lagos in the House of Assembly in Lagos.

The late Mr. Magnus Williams, veteran politician, lawyer and commentator summed up the House of Assembly event: "They went in peace but returned in pieces"

As against all of the above, the newly-formed Action Group was strong disciplined, cohesive, committed and well organized.

Because of time constraints, the Action Group concentrated on the West and limited its operations to that Region throughout the period of the country-wide elections.

The AG's campaign strategy was more effective. While the NCNC sought votes from important towns, the Action Group covered all grounds – towns, villages and hamlets. Above all, the Action Group came out with impressive and well-reasoned policy papers informing the voters of the programs which the party would pursue if elected.

It chose to work for a welfare state which would, among others, provide free education and free health service for the people.

Its motto, was: "Freedom for all and life more abundant". The NCNC did not present any policy papers. All the above reasons contributed not a little to the victory of the Action Group at the polls in 1951.

10

Why many believed NCNC's False claims.

FROM ALL THE facts disclosed in this work, I am confident that all fair-minded people would agree that the Action Group won the 1951 Parliamentary elections in the West. Why then were the false claims of the NCNC leaders believed by many Nigerians? There were three main reasons, in my view, for this.

The first had to do with the popularity of Dr. Azikiwe. He was at that time the most popular political figure in the country – the darling of the masses. Any story favorable to him or that could add more feathers to his cap the masses were ready to believe. It was also not easy for many people to believe that Zik and his NCNC could be worsted in any electoral battle at that time.

The second reason why the NCNC's false claims in respect of the election were and are still believed by many is that the falsehood is repeated *ad nauseam et infinitum.* Those who made the false claims had and have been Geobbelic and Mchiavellian in their tactics. That is why most of those who have bought the lies continue to repeat them even though they have no proof.

The third and last reason is the influence of Zik's chain of newspapers. They had done their best to plant these false claims in the minds of the people. It would be recalled that when Dr. Azikiwe returned to Nigeria from Ghana in 1937; he began the setting up of a chain of newspapers to promote his ideas. The newspapers were as follows:

West African Pilot – started publication on 22 November 1937, in Lagos.

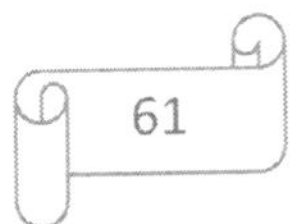

Easter Nigerian Guardian – hit the newsstands in Port Harcourt on 8 February 1940. The late A.K. Blankson was its first editor.

Nigerian Spokesman – linked up with the chain in 1943 at Onitsha, had the late Justice Olujide Somolu as its first editor.

Southern Nigerian Defender – joined the stable in Warri in the same year (1943) with Mr. G.U.M. Gardener and Tony Enahoro as its editors. This newspaper subsequently moved its base to Ibadan.

The Comet – a weekly, was purchased by Zik from Duse Mohamed Ali and turned into *Daily Comet,* became part of the newspaper empire in Lagos in 1944. Chief Enahoro was its first editor.

Eastern Sentinel – another daily, came on board on 15 December 1955 in Enugu under the editorial leadership of J.A.C. Onwuegbuna.

Nigerian Monitor – brought up the rear from Uyo in October 1960 with Samuel U. Okonko as its editor.

All these newspapers, now defunct, assisted by the other Zik and NCNC inclined ones and with the cooperation of many journalists who had passed through Zik's journalistic desk and were sympathetic to his cause did a lot to sell, either mischievously or as innocent agents, the wrong notion that Zik with his party, was robbed of victory in the 1951 Western elections.

He was not robbed of victory. Awo and his Action Group won the victory and as part of the oath taken in the witness box in court by a witness says that "is the truth, the whole truth and nothing but the truth".

Epilogue

BEFORE I CONCLUDE, It is necessary to remind readers that the main purpose of this work was to prove conclusively that it was Awo that won the first parliamentary election in the West in 1951 and not Zik. I am satisfied that this has been achieved. By way of emphasis, however, I like to recap some of the salient points put across in this book to prove my case.

At the close of the election on 24 September 1951, the Action Group judging by its list of candidates released before the election, had won 38 out of the 72 seats contested. Three days later, three AG scribes who contested as independents and won joined forces with their colleagues to sign the AG pacts of loyalty. The AG scribes were Alhaji D.S. Adegbenro (Egba Division), J.O. Oshuntokun (Ekiti Division) and S.O. Hassan (Epe Division).

Two of the 38 AG-sponsored members who were successful could not be reached to sign the pacts before they were sent for publication early in October 1951. The two legislators – R.A. Olusa (Owo Division) and C.A. Tewe (Okitipupa Division) subsequently associated with their colleague. If these two gentlemen had signed before publication the number of signatories to the pacts would have been 41 instead of 39 as published on 11 October 1951.

On 1 November 1951, Hon. T. Adeola Odutola's alignment with the Action Group was made known by Chief Bode Thomas through the *Daily Times* issue of that day. Chief Odutola contested and won as an independent but would have won on any platform in Ijebu Ode all the same.

On 6 December 1951 the Treasurer of the Action Group and General Secretary of the Benin provincial branch of the party topped the polls in Benin division. He, S.O. Ighodaro and two others won as members of Otu Edo.

More importantly, five of the six Ibadan People's party legislators after clearance with their party joined the Action Group.

There were, in all, 80 elected members in the Western House of Assembly.

Dr. Azikiwe, the leader of the NCNC was, at all material times, before the election confident of a landslide victory at the polls. For example the *Daily Times* of 20 September 1951 contained a report of a meeting of his party at the Glover Memorial Hall, Lagos, at which he told his members and supporters that the NCNC would win 50 or 60 seats in the pending Western elections. That was less than a week to the elections.

In his autobiography titled *"My Odyssey"*, Dr. Azikiwe sought to defend his abysmally poor performance at the polls. He told the world that he and his party were under the 'impression', that they had won 43 out of the 80 seats in the Western House of Assembly but 20 of the legislators whom they regarded as "members, supporters or sympathizers" aligned themselves with the Action group. He gave 16 names of those legislators which included:

(a) Chief Arthur Prest
(b) Chief Anthony Enahoro
(c) Four of the six IPP members in Ibadan
(d) One Coker of Oyo division
(e) Chief R.A. Olusa, C.A. Tewe and Rev. G.M. Fisher

The last three names mentioned above were on the list of AG-sponsored candidates and I do not think it is necessary to comment further on them since there were no facts to connect them with the NCNC.

As regards (d) above, there was no Coker among the five Oyo legislators of the period. There must have been a mix-up somewhere.

The Oyo legislators of 1951 were Bode Thomas, Abiodun Akerele, A.B.P. Martins, T.A. Amao and S.B. Eyitayo. Maybe a one-time political colleague of the NCNC leader could be of help to explain this apparent mix-up.

On (c) above, the elder statesman gave the names of four of the five Ibadan legislators who were given the clearance to align with the Action Group by their party, the IPP.

The only name Zik did not mention was S.A. Akinyemi, a retired policeman who left the force just in time to contest the election.

The Ibadan legislators contested and won on the platform of their local party. They were independent of both the Action Group and the NCNC.

After the election, Zik in particular and NCNC in general did their best to win them over but failed. Only Alhaji Adegoke Adelabu went with the NCNC.

Chief Anthony Enahoro who could be described as the builder of the AG in Ishan Division, was one of the moving spirits of the party in the Midwest.

On 14 April 1951, he was elected General Secretary of the Midwest zone of the party. He attended the joint conference of the party at Owo, where on 29 April 1951, he was elected the Assistant General Secretary.

In addition, the name Anthony Enahoro was conspicuous on the list of Action Group candidates made public before the election.

As regards Chief Arthur Prest, he was one of those who formed the Action group in Warri province in particular and the Midwest in general. He was elected the chairman of the party in the Midwest on 14 April 1951 in Sapele. The news media covered the event adequately.

More importantly, at the Owo conference of the party on 29 April 1951, he became a vice-chairman of the Action Group.

Furthermore, his name was on the list of candidates of the party published before the elections.

In view of all the above facts which were well-publicized, how could the NCNC say that they regarded leaders like Arthur Prest, Anthony Enahoro and others as "members, supporters or sympathizers" of their party until after the elections in September 1951?

I like to conclude by asking the NCNC leaders one important question: why did they neglect or refuse to publish the list of their candidates for the elections that took place in the West on 24 September 1951?

Appendix 1

Election Result Chart

Division	No of seats	Action Group	IND./AG	NCNC	IND./NCNC
1 Aboh	2	-	-	2	-
2 Asaba	3	-	-	3	-
3 Badagry	2	2	-	-	-
4 Benin	3	-	1	-	2
5 Egba	5	4	1	-	-
6 Egbado (now Yewa)	3	3	-	-	-
7 Ekiti	4	2	1	1	-
8 Epe	2	1	1	-	-
9 Ibadan	6	-	5	-	1
10 Ife	2	2	-	-	-
11 Ijebu-Ode	3	2	1	-	-
12 Ijebu-Remo	2	2	-	-	-
13 Ijesa	3	-	1	2	-
14 Ikeja	2	2	-	-	-
15 Ishan	2	1	-	1	-
16 Kukuruku (now Afenmai)	2	-	1	1	-
17 Lagos	5	-	-	5	-
18 Okitipupa	2	1	-	1	-
19 Ondo	2	-	2	-	-
20 Osun	7	7	-	-	-
21 Owo	3	2	-	1	-
22 Oyo	5	5	-	-	-
23 Urhobo	6	-	1	5	-
24 Warri	2	1	-	1	-
25Western Ijaw	2	1	-	1	-
Total	80	38	15	24	3

Appendix 2

Akanbi Olabode Thomas (1919-1953)

AKANBI OLABODE THOMAS simply and fondly called Bode Thomas, was born in Lagos, on Tuesday 17 October 1919. His illustrious and prosperous father was Andrew Wilkinson Thomas, an auctioneer and general merchant of Anikantamo District of Okepopo area of Lagos, who died in 1925. Bode's mother was Madam Sariyu Afinni, a beloved daughter of Imam Buraimo Amodu Afinni, a Prince merchant and Otun Balogun of Lagos. Madam Sariyu was also related to the Durosinmi-Etti family of Lagos.

After his father's death, Bode came under the guardianship of the late Mr. James George, the father of lady Ayodele Alakija who was a Justice of the Peace and solicitor of the Supreme Court of Nigeria. This fact had great influence on Bode's choice of profession. He was boarded by his guardian with Archdeacon J Olumide Lucas.

After his elementary education, Bode went to the CMS Grammar School, Lagos, from where he passed out in 1938. He decided to work for some time and got a job at the Nigerian Railways where he was earning two shillings a day.

He resigned his job and left for the UK to read law in 1939. While in the UK, he took an interest in student politics and he was one of the West African Students' Union members who passed a resolution in 1941 demanding internal self-government for Nigeria.

On completion of his course of studies, he returned to Nigeria in 1942 after being called to the Bar. Bode first of all set up a private practice on his own before he and his other two secondary schoolmates, F.R.A. Williams and R.A. Fani-

Kayode formed the legal firm of Thomas, Williams and Kayode. He was the senior partner of the firm.

In 1949, Olabode became the Balogun of the ancient town of Oyo, while in 1951 he was appointed the Chancellor of the African Church Organization.

In the same year, he was elected first member for Oyo Division in the Western House of Assembly. In January 1952, he became a member of the House of Representatives.

Later that year he was appointed Federal Minister of Transport and later that of Works. Before then, he had been General Secretary of the Action Group and Deputy Leader of its Parliamentary Council. He was a loyal, committed and active member.

Bode Thomas died on Friday 20 November 1953 at the young age of 34 years following a brief illness.